THIS BOOK BELONGS TO:

CONTACT INFORMATION

NAME:	
ADDRESS:	
PHONE:	

START / END DATES

___ / ___ / ___   TO   ___ / ___ / ___

Be Your Own HERO

Table of Contents

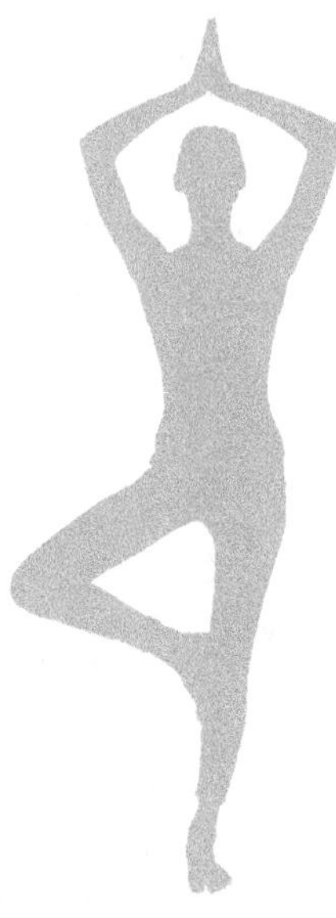

STAY UP TO DATE ON FUTURE BOOKS & DEALS

SCAN THE QR CODE BELOW TO BE INCLUDED IN FUTURE BOOKS, SPECIALS DEALS, DISCOUNTS, AND FREE GIVEAWAYS! SIMPLY SCAN BELOW WITH YOUR CELL PHONE AND CLICK ON ENTER EMAIL ADDRESS TAB AND WE WILL DO THE REST. THAT'S IT!

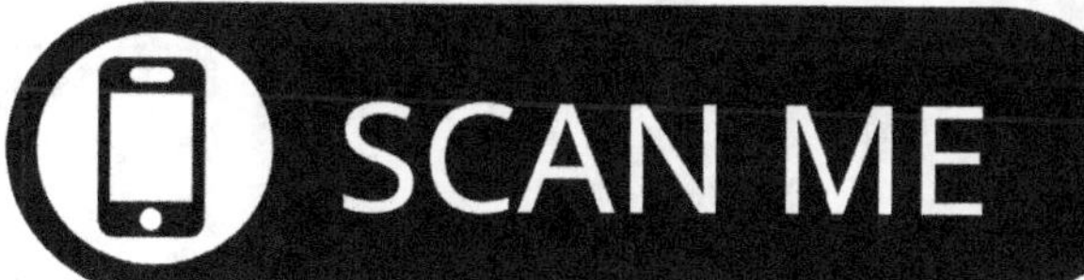

IDEAS AND NOTES

Name: ___________________________

Getting Started

Whether you're looking to transform your mood, improve flexibility, strength and posture, or you're simply interested in increasing energy and slimming down, yoga offers all of these advantages and many more.

The best thing about yoga is that it doesn't take a lot of time out of your day. In fact, if you can spare just 15 minutes, you can reap the benefits and rewards that come with integrating this mind & body practice into your daily routine.

So are you ready to learn the top yoga poses that will help you improve your health, lose weight, and live a better, more positive life?

Let's begin!

Top Poses to Reduce Stress

We all deal with stress and anxiety in our daily lives. Whether it comes from business or personal relationships, learning how to effectively cope with anxiety and manage stress levels is an important role in living a happy and successful life.

Yoga is also a powerful tool at helping to channel negative energy from your body so that you can **reset your mind and spirit** so that you're focused on remaining calm and relaxed.

In addition, these poses will help you to experience an increase in energy and focus while decreasing tension.

Eagle Pose:

This pose will test your balance and core strength.

Step 1: Begin by standing in the mountain pose with your feet together and your knees slightly bent.

You could also choose to start in a chair position where you are sitting deeply within the pose right from the beginning.

Step 2: Shift your weight onto your left foot and cross your right thigh over your left. If you can hook your right foot behind your left calf, go for it! If not, don't worry. You'll still gain all the benefits of this strengthening pose.

Step 3: Cross your left elbow over your right and bring the palms of your hands together.

Step 4: Squeeze your legs together and sit back as if sitting in a chair. Life your elbows to shoulder height and reach your hands forward away from you to really feel that stretch.

If you feel comfortable, you can bow slightly forward and bring the bottom of your elbow to the top of your knee.

Here's another pose to help you eliminate stress and anxiety:

Child's Pose:

This is a great pose to help you relax but it's also a fantastic resting position in between more intense transitions.

Step 1: Start on your hands and knees. Inhale deeply and begin to clear your mind of all thoughts. Listen to your breathing.

Step 2: Spread your knees apart while keeping both big toes touching. Rest your buttocks on your heels comfortably.

Step 3: Sit up straight to lengthen and stretch your spine. Now, exhale, bow forward, moving your torso in between your thighs. Let your forehead touch the floor.

Step 4: Keep your arms extended and stretched with your palms facing down as you press back slightly with your hands, maintaining contact with your buttocks and your heels. Keep your eyes closed as you breathe in, breathe out.

Step 5: Hold for a minute or longer. To release, use your hands to walk your torso back into an upright, sitting position.

Improving Flexibility

Increasing flexibility goes hand in hand with enhancing your range of motion and improving the overall health of your joints, which in turn will work towards eliminating back and shoulder pain.

Improving your flexibility will also help you get more out of your workouts. In fact, flexibility is a **core component to proper physical fitness** because it plays a major role in your ability to increase range of motion and being able to complete a high-intensity workout routine effectively.

The key is to start off slow and steady. Instead of rushing into advanced poses that you may not be ready for, you'll want to start off with a **series of simple poses** that supports muscle-building while helping you learn correct posture and safe alignment during your routine.

Here are a couple of poses to help you get started:

Eye of the Needle

This is a great pose for stretching out your hips and building your flexibility in a smooth and gentle way.

Step 1: Start by lying on your back with your knees bent and the soles of your feet flat on the floor.

Step 2: Next, place your right ankle on top of your left thigh while opening your right knee.

Step 3: Lift your left foot from the floor slowing and start to bring your left thigh towards your chest.

Step 4: Reach your right hand through the space between your legs in order to clasp your hands around the back of your left thigh.

Step 5: Bring your left knee towards your chest as close as you feel comfortable with.

Step 6: After 5-6 breaths, switch legs and repeat.

Another great pose for improving flexibility is one of the most popular foundational poses:

The Downward Facing Dog

Here's the right way to complete this pose:

Step 1: Start with your hands and knees on the floor in a comfortable position with your buttocks pointed out and slightly up.

Step 2: Next, place your knees directly below your hips and your hands slightly forward (towards your shoulders). Spread the palms of your hands out on the floor and turn your toes under.

Step 3: Lift your knees up by curling your toes under as you move. Straighten your knees, draw your thighs back and lift your legs higher. Reach your heels down.

Step 4: Hold this position ensuring that your arms are straight and your thighs are pressed back, elongating your spine. Breathe in deeply and smoothly.

Step 5: Lower your knees to the floor to release the position.

Instant Energy Boost

Are you often finding it hard to stay focused and alert throughout the day? Need a quick pick-me-up without the caffeine?

Just a few minutes of yoga each day can give you that instant energy boost that gets you through the day.

Here are a few of our top energy-boosting yoga poses:

Tree Pose

This pose helps energy circulate throughout your body while opening your chest.

The tree pose also works to stretch your shoulders, torso and thighs while building strength in your calves and legs. And when it comes to boosting your energy, the tree pose will do that and more, including improving your focus and concentration.

Here's how to do this foundational pose:

Step 1: Begin by standing with your feet together, inner ankles and knees touching.

Step 2: Bring your hands together at the center of your chest. Exhale deeply, focusing on the pose.

Step 3: Shift your weight onto your right foot, then bend your left knee and move it upwards. Keep your spine stretched, reach down and clasp your left ankle. Place the sole of your left foot on your inner right thigh.

Step 4: Stand tall, keeping your focus on the wall in front of you in a straight line.

Step 5: Press your left foot into your inner right thigh while pressing your right thigh into your foot to strength your core and improve your balance.

Step 6: If you feel balanced, raise your arms above your head with your palms together. Breathe and hold for 5-8 breaths.

Step 7: Release, slowing exhaling while bring your arms down. Release your legs.

Step 8: Repeat on the other side.

"Like a tree, extend your roots down and blossom your arms up towards the sun. The stronger the roots, the taller the tree." -
Baron Baptiste

Tip: If you struggle with the tree pose, consider bringing your arms out to the sides for additional stability.

You can also use a wall to practice, placing one free hand on the wall for support.

The Cobra Pose

This pose will open your chest and strengthen your core while giving you an instant energy boost.

Here's how to do it:

Step 1: Start by lying on your stomach, chin rested on the floor and your palms flat, tucked under your shoulders. Keep your legs together.

Step 2: Pull up your knees, squeezing your thighs and pressing your pubic bone down into the floor.

Step 3: Without using your arms for support, inhale and lift your chest and head from the floor. Make sure to keep your neck in line with your spine.

Step 4: Keeping your elbows close to your sides, press down into the palms of your hands using only your arms to lift you. Drop your shoulders down and back while pressing your chest forward.

Step 5: Breathe and hole for 3-5 breaths.

Step 6: Release, exhaling and lowering your chest and head to the floor slowly and evenly.

And here's one more to help re-energize you!

The Locust Pose

This is a core pose so you'll want to learn it early so you can incorporate it into your daily routine.

The locust pose strengthens your legs and tones your body while helping to stretch your lower back.

Step 1: Begin by lying on your stomach, chin on the floor and your legs and arms placed alongside your body. Keep your palms facing down.

Step 2: Pull up your knees, squeezing your buttocks and thighs as you pull and press your pubic bone down to the floor like you did with the cobra pose.

Step 3: Inhale deeply, lifting your legs, chest, head and arms from the floor. Reach out, keeping your neck in line with your spine.

Step 4: Drop your shoulders down, and press your chest forward slowly. Keep your buttocks and legs strong.

Step 5: Breathe and hold for 2-5 breaths.

Step 6: Release, exhaling slowing, lowering your head, arms, legs and chest to the floor.

Fat Burning Poses

If you're looking to shed fat, tone up your body and strengthen your core in order to reduce back pain, tighten up your abs and get fit, then you'll want to give these powerful fat-burning yoga poses a try.

Many people are surprised to discover just how effective yoga can be at helping you lose weight but keep this in mind: muscle burns more calories than fat, right?

And with yoga, you are building muscle mass through a series of regular strength and balance based activities. By incorporating yoga into your day, your muscles will also begin to lengthen and tone, which helps you look slimmer!

And yoga helps support weight loss in yet another powerful way. It works towards relieving pressure and tension and helping you find balance and clarity in your life. An uplift in your mood and a practice that supports discipline and mindfulness will make it easier for you to stay on track with your weight loss goals!

Here are a couple of yoga poses to help you get started:

Upward-Facing Dog Pose

Note: *You shouldn't practice Upward-Facing Dog pose if you have carpal tunnel syndrome or recent back or wrist injury without first consulting with your doctor.*

Step 1: Begin by lying face-down on the floor. Extend your legs behind you, spread a few inches apart. The top of your feet should rest on your mat.

Step 2: Place your hands on the floor alongside your body, next to your lower ribs. Keep your elbows tugged into the side of your body and your fingers pointed to the top of your mat.

Step 3: Inhale deeply as you press your hands firmly to the floor. Straighten your arms, slowly lifting your torso and legs just a few inches from the floor.

Step 4: Press down firmly through the tops of your feet. You'll feel your leg muscles engage.

The objective is to keep your thighs lifted away from the floor. Keep your elbows tucked alongside your body as you drop your shoulders and lift your chest towards the ceiling. You can either keep your head neutral or gaze upwards if you're comfortable.

Step 5: Hold the pose for up to 40 seconds. To release, exhale as you lower your torso slowly and place your forehead to your mat.

Upward Plank Pose

Step 1: Begin by sitting with your hands placed a few inches behind your hips with your fingers pointing forward.

Step 2: Bend your knees and place your feet flat on the floor, big toes turned inward and heels placed at least a foot away from your buttocks.

Step 3: Begin with a deep exhale, then press your inner feet and hands down against the floor.

Step 4: Lift your hips until you come into a reverse tabletop position, with your thighs and torso parallel to the floor.

Your Daily Routine

As you learn different poses, feel free to switch things up and add different routines into your weekly schedule.

In addition, the more flexible you become, the longer you'll be able to hold the poses or the more challenging you can make them!

Pose #1:

The Downward Facing Dog

Step 1: Start with your hands and knees on the floor in a comfortable position with your buttocks pointed out and slightly up.

Step 2: Next, place your knees directly below your hips and your hands slightly forward (towards your shoulders). Spread the palms of your hands out on the floor and turn your toes under.

Step 3: Lift your knees up by curling your toes under as you move. Straighten your knees, draw your thighs back and lift your legs higher. Reach your heels down.

Step 4: Hold this position ensuring that your arms are straight and your thighs are pressed back, elongating your spine. Breathe in deeply and smoothly.

Step 5: Lower your knees to the floor to release the position.

Pose #2

The Locust Pose

Step 1: Begin by lying on your stomach, chin on the floor and your legs and arms placed alongside your body. Keep your palms facing down.

Step 2: Pull up your knees, squeezing your buttocks and thighs as you pull and press your pubic bone down to the floor like you did with the cobra pose.

Step 3: Inhale deeply, lifting your legs, chest, head and arms from the floor. Reach out, keeping your neck in line with your spine.

Step 4: Drop your shoulders down, and press your chest forward slowly. Keep your buttocks and legs strong.

Step 5: Breathe and hold for 2-5 breaths.

Step 6: Release, exhaling slowing, lowering your head, arms, legs and chest to the floor.

Pose #3:

Tree Pose

Step 1: Begin by standing with your feet together, inner ankles and knees touching.

Step 2: Bring your hands together at the center of your chest. Exhale deeply, focusing on the pose.

Step 3: Shift your weight onto your right foot, then bend your left knee and move it upwards. Keep your spine stretched, reach down and clasp your left ankle. Place the sole of your left foot on your inner right thigh.

Step 4: Stand tall, keeping your focus on the wall in front of you in a straight line.

Step 5: Press your left foot into your inner right thigh while pressing your right thigh into your foot to strength your core and improve your balance.

Step 6: If you feel balanced, raise your arms above your head with your palms together. Breathe and hold for 5-8 breaths.

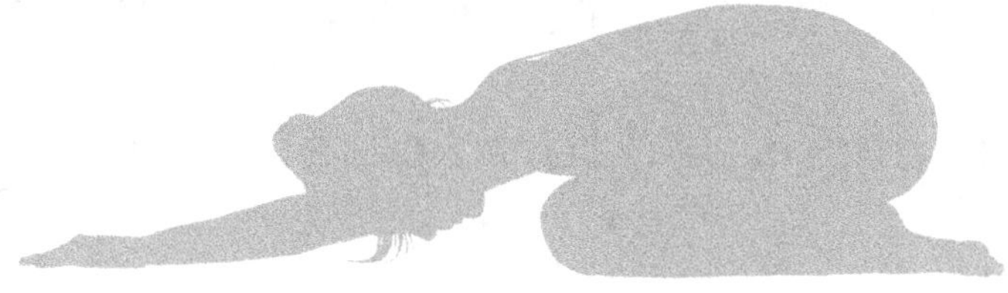

Step 7: Release, slowing exhaling while bring your arms down. Release your legs.

Step 8: Repeat on the other side.

Upward Plank Pose

Step 1: Begin by sitting with your hands placed a few inches behind your hips with your fingers pointing forward.

Step 2: Bend your knees and place your feet flat on the floor, big toes turned inward and heels placed at least a foot away from your buttocks.

Step 3: Begin with a deep exhale, then press your inner feet and hands down against the floor.

Step 4: Lift your hips until you come into a reverse tabletop position, with your thighs and torso parallel to the floor.

Final Words

Yoga offers so many benefits to your everyday life and since it only takes a few minutes each day, it's easy to stay focused and on track.

In addition to all the benefits we've discussed in this special report, such as reducing stress, improving overall mental health and supporting weight loss, yoga also is known to decrease the risk of heart disease while reducing the pace of your breathing which is linked to a longer life span!

And if you've ever found yourself suffering from insomnia, yoga can help you get a sound night's sleep.

There's no better or easier way to set yourself on a path towards ongoing happiness, mental clarity and health than by incorporating yoga into your everyday life.

Remember, the key is consistency. The more often you work towards setting aside just a few minutes each day to do these poses, the faster you'll be able to create a lifetime habit that will keep you energized, calm and centered. You deserve it!

I hope this report helps you get started on a path towards mindfulness, inner peace and improved health.

To a happy journey ahead!

For Advanced Technics Make Sure And Pick Up Your Hero Pilates Ring & Bar

PILATES HERO RING

1 Lying on the yoga mat,
set the circle between your legs,
squeeze hard,relax legs

2 According to the last step,
lift your body,hand joints bracing,
relaxing,legs squeeze hard

3 Raised your body slightly,lift arms,
open legs,set the circle between
your legs and squeeze

4 According to the last step,
lift your legs and squeeze,
take a deep breath

5 Side lying on the yoga mat,
one hand support,set the circle
between your legs and squeeze hard

6 According to the last step,
lift your legs and squeeze,
take a deep breath

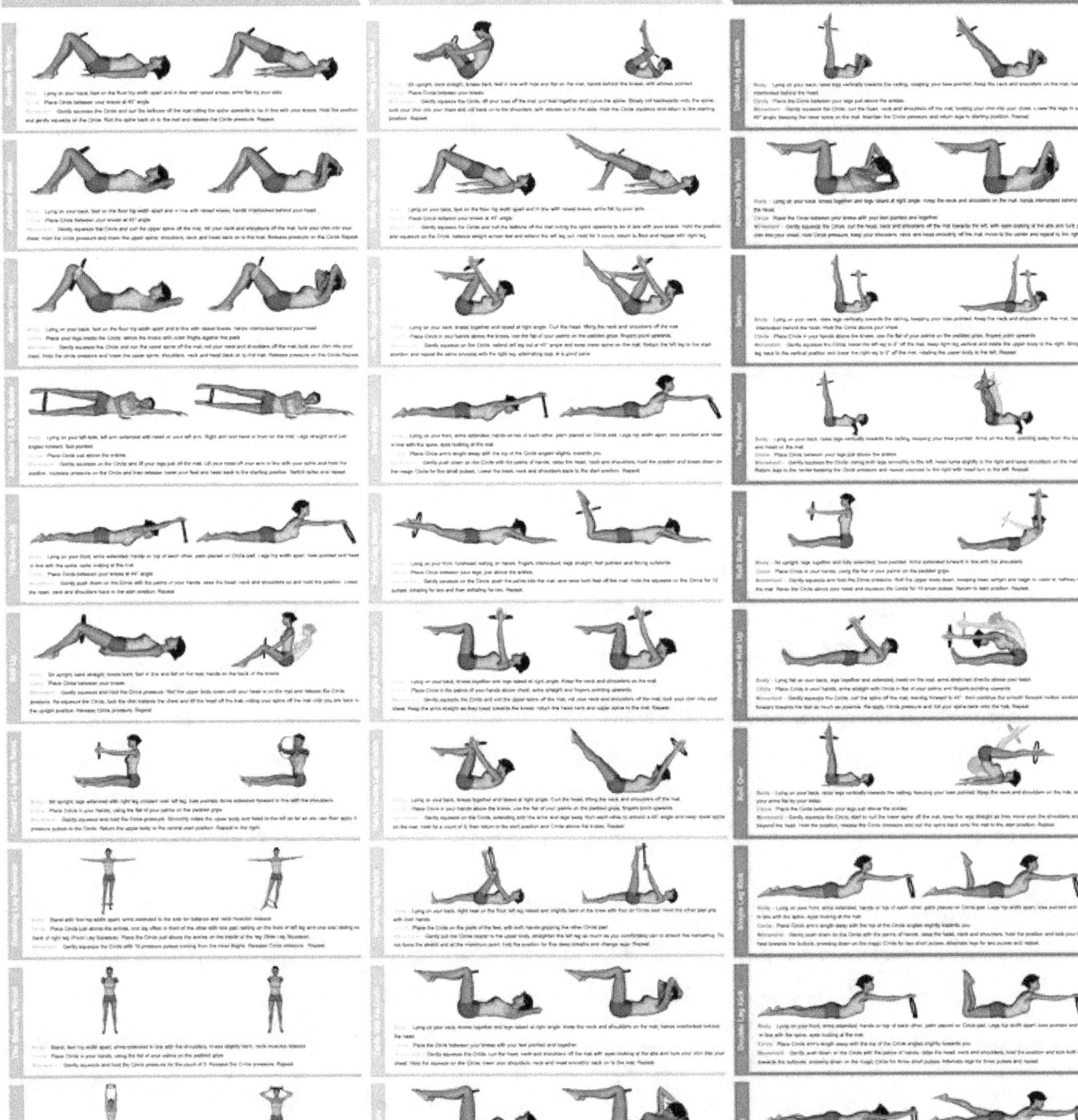

PILATES HERO RING
BEGINNER
INTERMEDIATE
ADVANCED

PILATES HERO RING

1   3x6-10   30"

N°2   3x30"   30"

3   3x6-10   30"

N°4   3x6-10   30"

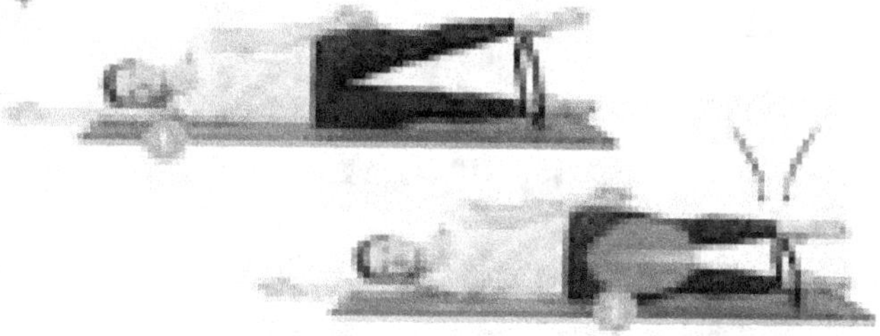

5   3x6-10   30"

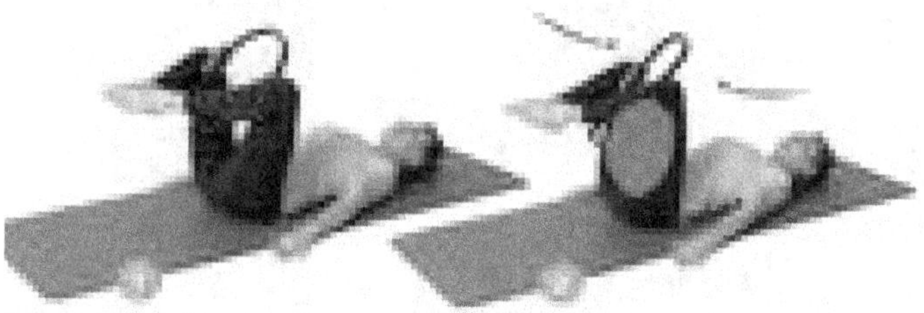

N°6   3x6-10   30"

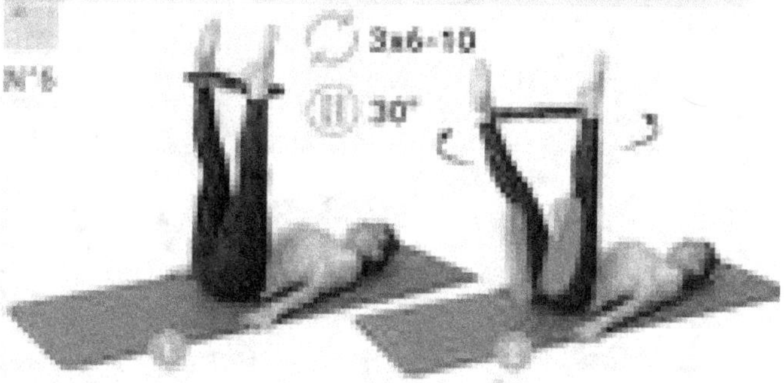

7   3x30"   30"

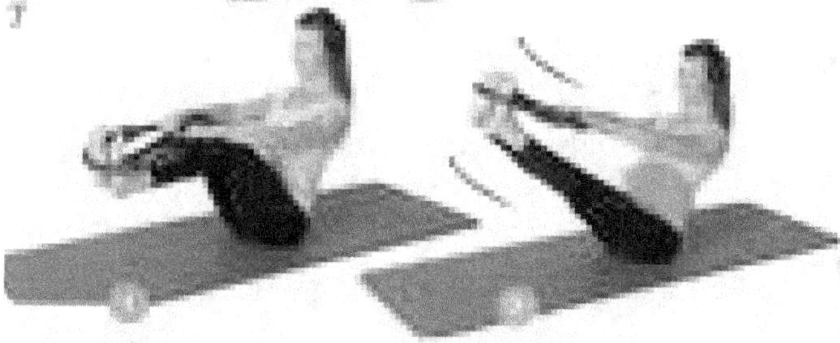

N°8   3x6-10   30"

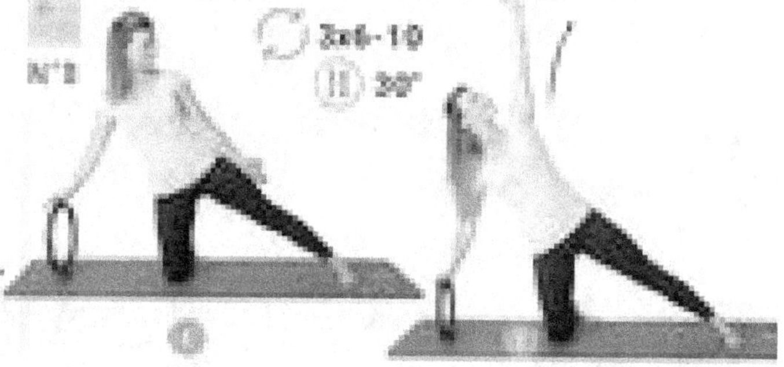

9   3x6-10   30"

HERO

1.Walking Stretch

2.Barbell Exercise

3.Waist Twisting

4.Squat Exercise

5.Bridge Stretch

6.Leg Stretching

7.Leg Lifting

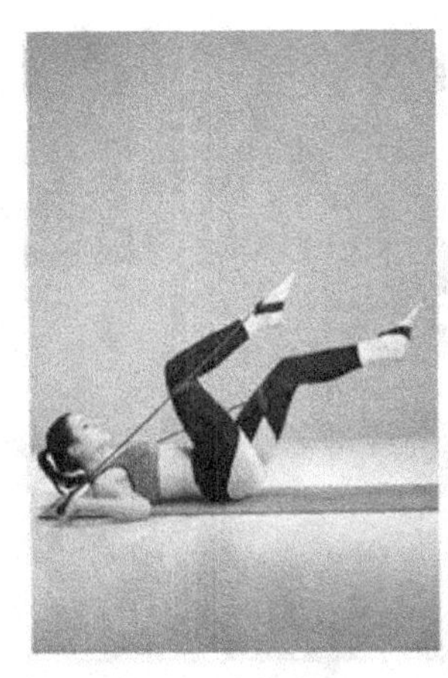

8.Cycling in the Air

PILATES HERO BAR

1.Walking Stretch   2.Barbell Exercise   3.Waist Twisting   4.Squat Exercise

5.Bridge Stretch   6.Leg Stretching   7.Leg Lifting   8.Cycling in the Air

PILATES HERO BAR

LOW IMPACT, HIGH RESULTS

PILATES HERO BAR

PILATES *HERO* BAR

6. Upright row

7. "Good morning"

8. Biceps curl

Lower Body Workout

9. Squat

10. Leg extension

11. Abduction

12. Squat with the stick held above your head

13. Lunge in a step position with body rotation

Link for Bar

14. Calf raise

15. Straight leg dead lift

16. Rear lunge
(both loops in the front foot)

Mid Section Workout

17. Standing body rotation

18. Forward leaning body rotation

19. Crunch or sit-up with biceps curl

20. Seated body rotation

21. Crunch or sit-up with upright row

22. Leg bends

23. Side bend

24. "Good morning"

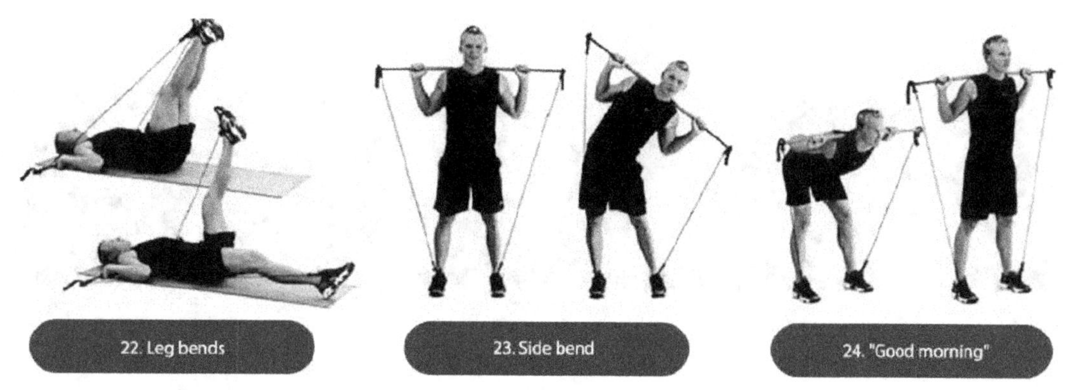

Stretching exercises

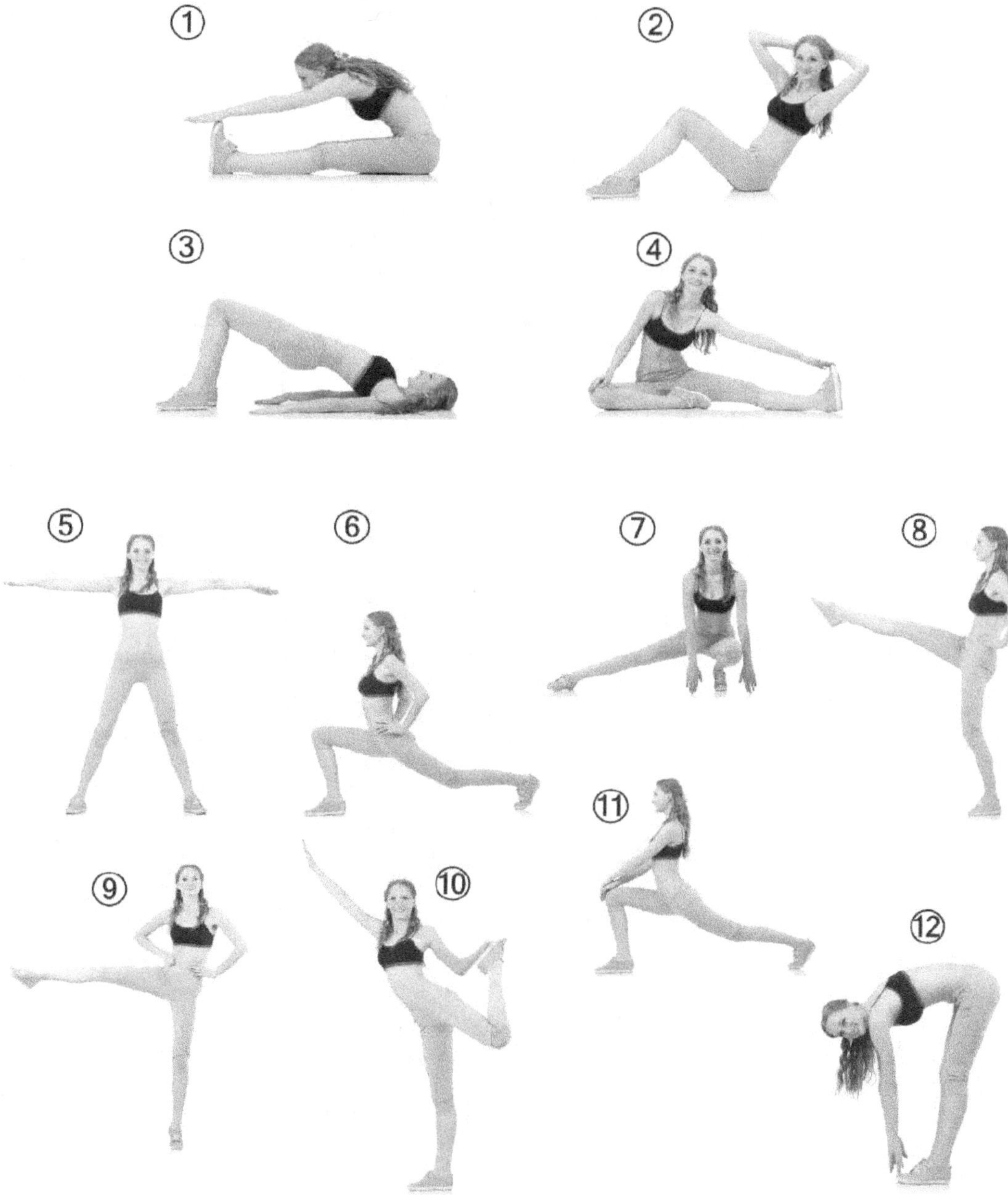
①
②
③
④
⑤
⑥
⑦
⑧
⑨
⑩
⑪
⑫

Exercise 1

Objective: Exercising the biceps.

Posture: Set your feet shoulder width apart and press the stretch band to the floor with both feet.
Make sure that your back is straight!
Grip the training bar with both hands from below, keeping your hands shoulder width apart, and hold it horizontally at hip height.

Exercise: Pull your forearms and hands slowly towards the upper body.
Keep your elbows close to the upper body.
Keep your shoulders down!
Return to the starting position.

Breathing: Exhale when you lift your arms, inhale when you lower them.

Repetitions: 15-20 times

Advanced variation: Set your feet further apart to increase the resistance of the stretch band.

 **Caution:** Position your feet between the markings on the stretch bands.

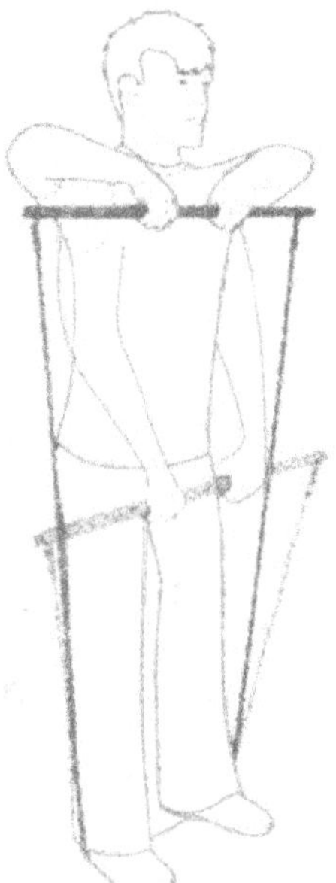

Exercise 2

Objective: Exercising the mid shoulder muscles.

Posture: Set your feet shoulder width apart and press the stretch band to the floor with both feet.
Make sure that your back is straight!
Grip the training bar with both hands from above, keeping your hands close together, and hold it horizontally at hip height.

Exercise: Pull the training bar slowly upwards, keeping it close to your body, until it reaches chest height.
Keep your shoulders down!
Return to the starting position.

Breathing: Exhale when you lift your ar ms, inhale when you lower them.

Repetitions: 15-20 times

For the advanced: Set your feet further apart to increase the resistance of the stretch band.

 **Caution:** Position your feet between the markings on the stretch bands.

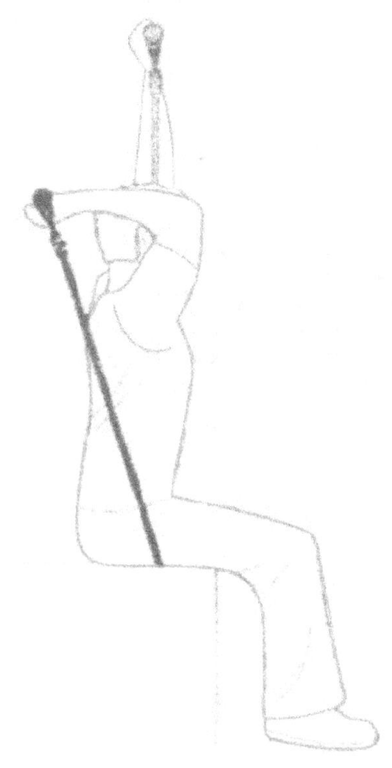

Exercise 3

Objective: Exercising the triceps.

Posture: Sit on a chair and fit the stretch band under your bottom.
Grip the training ba with both hands from above, keeping your hands shoulder width apart or closer.
Make sure that your back is straight!

Exercise: Start off with your arms stretched upwards.
DO not fully extend them!
Bend your arms backwards towards your neck.
Your elbows are to be kept tucked in; do not spread them apart!
Keep your shoulders down!

Breathing: Exhale when you lift your arms, inhale when you lower them.

Repetitions: 15-20 times

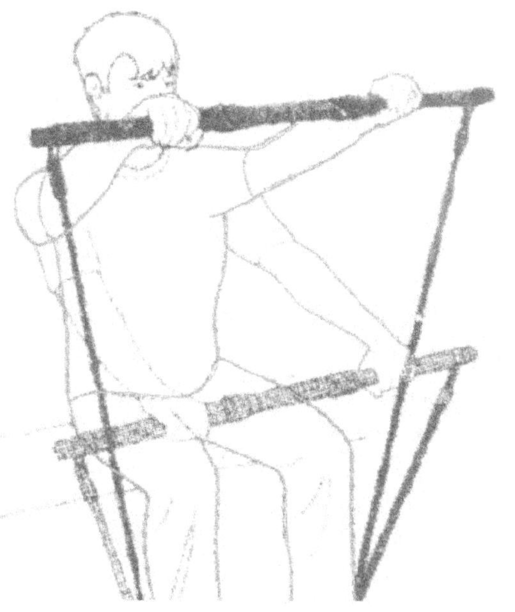

Exercise 4

Objective: Exercising the front shoulder muscles.

Posture: Sit on achair and fit the stretch band under your feet.
Grip the training bar with both hands from above, keeping your hands shoutder width apart. and hold it horizontally at hip height.
Make sure that your back is straight!

Exercise: Pull your stretched arms siowly up to head height.
Keep your shoulders down!
Return to the stating position.

Breathing: Exhale when you lift your arms, inhale when you lower them.

Repetitions: 15-20 times

Advanced variation: Pull your arins all the way up and over your head.

Exercise 5

Objective: Exercising leg muscles and lower back.

Posture: Set your feet parallel to each other, shoulder width apart.
and press the stretch band to the floor with both feet.
Grip the training bar with both hands from above, Keeping your
hands shoulder width apart. Lift the bar behind your head and place
it down on your shoulders.
Make sure that your back is straight!

Exercise: Do some slow squats.
Keep your back straight, push your bottom outwards to the rea,
weight On both your heels.

Breathing: inhale when you bend, exhale when you straighten up.

Repetitions: 15-20 times

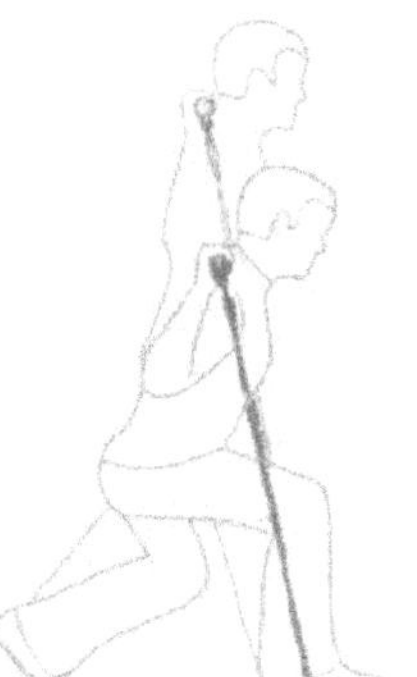

Variation: Move to a stepping position with the stretch band under
your front foot.

Objective: Additional exercising of the muscles in your bottom.

Exercise 6

Objective: Exercising the abdominal muscles.

Posture: Lie down on the floor on your back with your legs at a stight angie.
Place the stretch band under both feet.
Grip the training bar with both hands from below. keeping your hands shoulder width apart,
roughiy at hip height, so that some tension is exerted on the stretch band.

Exercise: Tense your abdominal muscles and slowly raise your upper body. Your head should remain in a
straight line as an extension of the spine. 00 not pull it down towards your chest!
Lower your upper body again, but do not lower your head. Remember to keep yourself tense!

Breathing: Exhale when you lift your arms, inhale when you lower them.

Repetitions: 15-20 times

Variation: Moving your forearms upwards at the same time makes sitting up stightly easier.
You can aiso choose a stretch band with greater puling force.

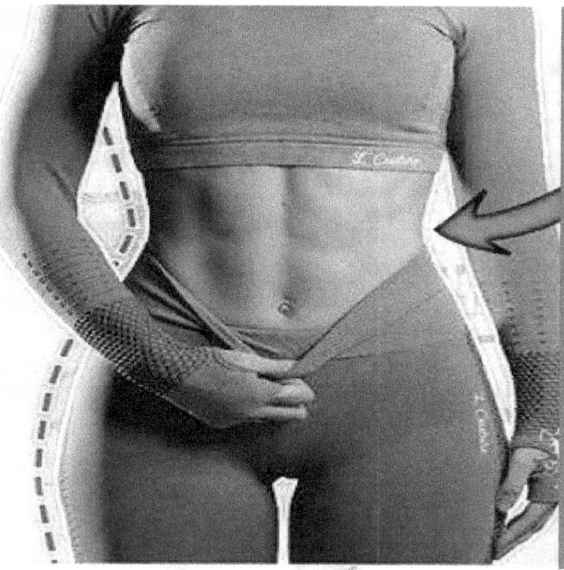

ULTIMATE AT HOME WORKOUT GUIDE!

1.
2.
3.
4.
5.
6.
7.
8.

PILATES HERO BAR

Link for Bar

Office Break Workout

1. Front aquat with one leg military press

2. Standing body rotation

3. Triceps press

4. Bar row

5. Abduction

PILATES HERO BAR

Be Your Own HERO

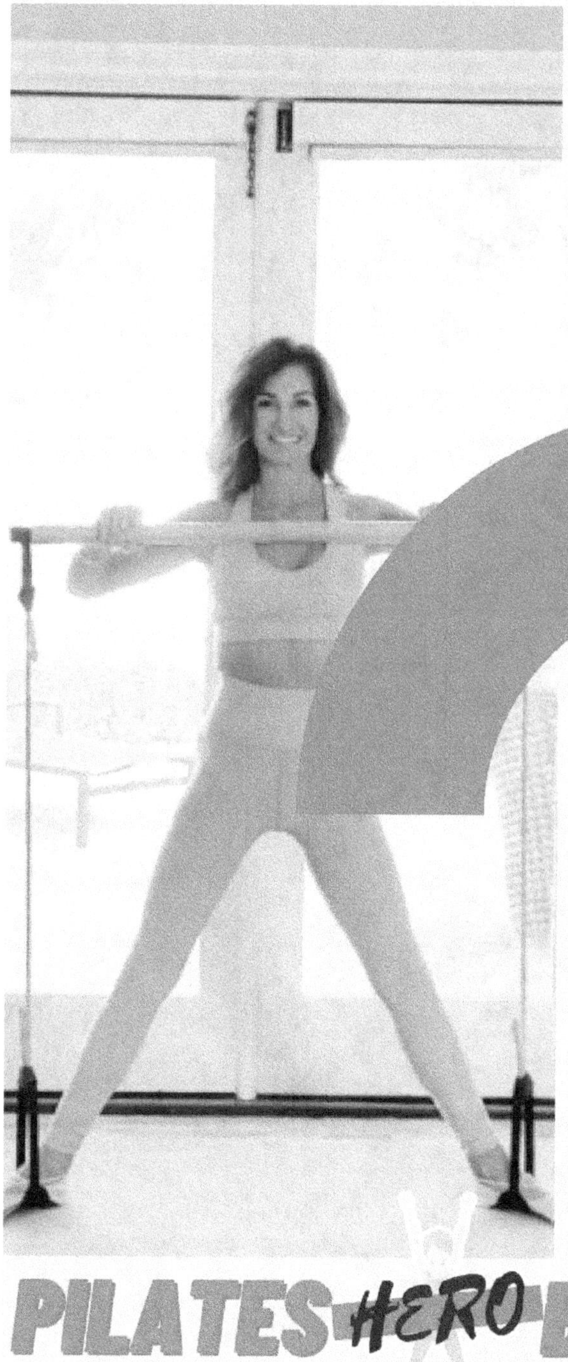

> We are what we repeatedly do. Excellence then is not an act but a habit.
>
> —Aristotle

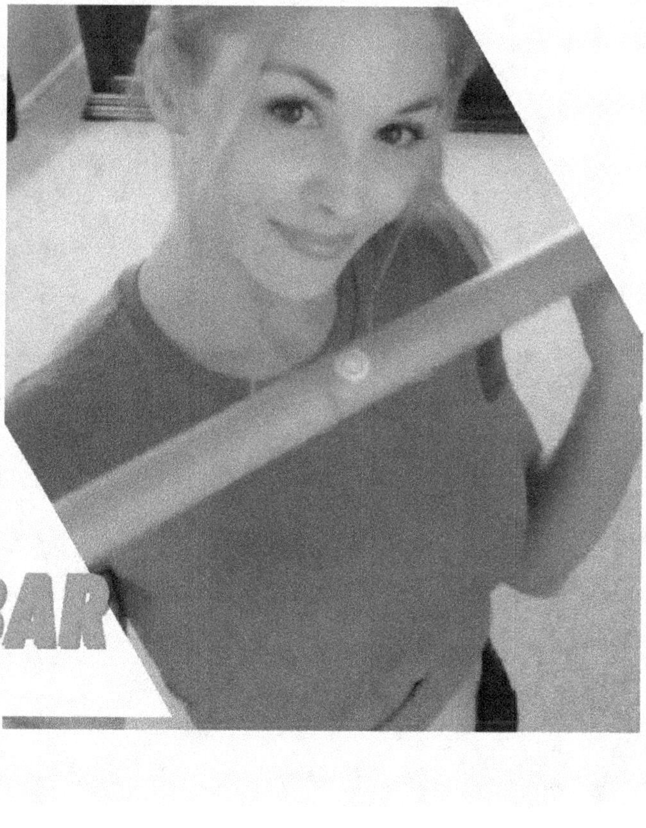